SHE WHO STANDS - SACRED AND UNTAMED

PRAGATI MISHRA

This book is under 100 pages because I know how much it means to actually finish a book. Sometimes, that feeling alone is everything.

Happy Reading.

I want to dedicate this book to women and people everywhere who've been told to be someone they're not. This is especially for my mother, Meera Mishra, and my aunts: Usha Dubey, Shakuntala Upadhyay, Shashikala Mishra, and Sunita Shukla, and all the strong women around me who've shown me that you don't have to let the tamed ones tell you how to live.

I also dedicate this to my father, the late Mr. Ramsahay Mishra. He may not be here physically anymore, but he's still with me — in my heart, in how I carry myself, in everything I do. He raised me to be untamed, sacred, and unapologetically myself. He always told me, "You're going to win." And I believed him. And I do.

To my brother, Harsh Mishra, thank you for always helping me move forward, for being my biggest support system, and for never letting me lose sight of myself.

And to my mentors Anup Talwar, Suren Kolkankar, and Prashant Bhandarkar, I'm so grateful. You've always kept me aligned with growth. You watched over me, gave me space when I needed it, and reminded me of who I am, even on the days I forgot.

This book is a little reminder to look again, rethink,
remix, and truly live.

Contents

Preface

I grew up a very curious, unconventional and fresh thinker, I had perspectives that would always be more about whys about the things and in my quest to find answers i have been open to learning alot. I upskilled myself in many ways - Rationally, Mentally & spiritually. I have always looked at being comfortable in the autihenticity that comes to me naturally and have been a promoter of living an unharmed untamed lives, where we just pause and question things sometimes to ensure we are living better than yesterday.

Lets dive into a story of perspective. Each chapter has perspective, each chapter has a takeway, each chapter has a mantra. It belongs to you.

I am a certified NLP Practitioner, Emotional Intelligence coach, I am a Vipassana practitioner, a Human. A good woman and wild soul. My Instagram is Her_OwnHero - because yeah damsel never was in distress.

Here's a perspective:

I once read a story where " Daughter Ana, and her mother Maria were cooking ham together, and the mother cut the ham from the back, Ana asked "Hey Ma! why do you do that? " Maria answered "thats how you do it". to which Ana questioned "Yeah but why do you do it like that?" Maria was confused as she did not have an answer to that and she decided to call her mother to check the same. Maria aked "Ma! why did you cut the ham from the back while cooking?" her mother said - "thats because my oven was only 12 inch long and usually the ham was bigger than that". Maria realised that even when she has a 20 inch oven she has been cutting the ham because she thought thats how its done"!

This isnt about Ham its about us not realisining what else have we just been doing. .

Lets Go!

Acknowledgements

I read & observe people alot and have picked up my observations and collated it together in the way it made sense to my map of the reality.

It is an acknowledgement that you have all somehow inspired me :)

Prologue

She Who Stands – Sacred and the Untamed

There is a hidden force within every woman. It doesn't always arrive with thunder. Sometimes, it shows up in silence in the pause between breaths, in the stillness after a storm, in the moments she almost forgets who she is.

It is Shakti. Ancient, wild, unapologetically alive.

It lives in the tension between what is sacred and what is untamed, between what we are told to be and what we already are.

This book is not a roadmap. It's a reckoning.

Not a guide, but a gentle nudge toward remembering.

Remembering the parts of you that existed before the world handed you names, labels, and expectations.

It's for the woman who's been everything to everyone and still feels like something's missing.

It's for the woman who's tired of explaining herself and ready to reclaim herself.

She who stands, not always loudly, but firmly.

She who is sacred, not because she is perfect, but because she is real.

She who is untamed, not because she is reckless, but because she refuses to be caged.

This is your reminder that within you lives a force both fierce and tender.

It will rise when you are ready.

And once it does, it won't ask for permission.

CHAPTER ONE

BREAKING THE CAGE

"The moment a woman decides she is enough, the world calls her too much."

Society had always been quick to define her—a daughter, a sister, a wife. Roles carved into the stone of expectation. Yet, the moment she dared to carve her own path, the whispers began: selfish, ungrateful, difficult.

Aradhana sits at a seemingly ordinary family dinner. The table is set, conversations flow, but beneath the surface lies the weight of unspoken rules. She feels the edges of the invisible cage tightening—a life defined by compliance, where she's expected to stay small and obedient.

The shift happens suddenly, ignited by a seemingly casual remark from her father: "Good daughters know their place." It's a phrase she has heard countless times, each time pressing her further into silence. But tonight, something snaps.

She raises her head and meets her father's gaze, her voice steady yet filled with an unfamiliar fire. "And where exactly is that place?"

The table falls silent. Her family's shocked expressions reveal what the words don't: Women don't ask these questions. They comply, they appease, they endure. But Aradhana refuses to play the part any longer.

She speaks—haltingly at first, then with growing confidence—about the dreams she abandoned, the identity she lost in her quest to be the "perfect" daughter. Her voice grows louder as she names the stifling roles forced upon her, the unyielding cultural norms, and the oppressive expectations that have shaped her life.

Her words ignite chaos. Her father's voice rises in protest, her mother's face flushes with disapproval, and her siblings look away, unable to meet her gaze. Accusations of disrespect and selfishness fly at her, but for the first time, Aradhana doesn't flinch. She doesn't apologize.

This is her moment of breaking the cage—a declaration that she will no longer be defined by others' comfort or confined by their expectations.

The Connection to Divine Feminine

Aradhana's defiance echoes the story of Goddess Kali, whose fiery energy embodies liberation and truth. Just as Kali's rage tore through illusions, Aradhana's confrontation dismantles the facade of harmony built on her silence. Kali is often misunderstood as destructive, but her power lies in her ability to clear the path for authenticity and transformation.

Aradhana begins to recognize her own divinity—the unapologetic feminine force within her that refuses to be diminished. Like Kali, she is not "too much"; she is enough, exactly as she is.

Reflection and Practical Takeaways

1. What roles or expectations feel like a cage to me?
2. Where have I silenced my voice to avoid being labeled as "too much"?
3. What would it mean to reclaim my truth, even if it disrupts others' comfort?

Mantra:
"I am not here to fit. I am here to be free."

CHAPTER TWO

THE WEIGHT OF EXPECTATIONS

"She carried the weight of worlds not meant for her shoulders, until she realized she was born to soar, not stoop."

The aftermath of Aradhana's defiance is not quiet. Her family, wounded by what they see as betrayal, reacts with a spectrum of emotions: anger, disappointment, and bewilderment. Her mother weeps, lamenting the loss of the "good daughter" she raised. Her father, hurt yet unable to articulate it, retreats into cold silence. Relatives, hearing of the confrontation, call to intervene, turning the issue into family gossip.

Despite the storm swirling around her, Aradhana feels an unfamiliar sensation—relief. For years, she had carried the invisible weight of compliance, sacrificing her desires and identity to keep the peace. But now, she sees clearly how suffocating this peace has been, a shackle disguised as harmony.

This chapter captures the duality of breaking free: the liberation that comes from choosing oneself and the discomfort of facing the world's disapproval.

Unpacking the Burden of Expectations

Through Aradhana's reflections, we delve deeper into the origins of the expectations that have shaped her life. Society's template for women is stark:

- Be nurturing, even at your own expense.
- Be agreeable, even when it means silencing your truth.
- Be selfless, even when it erases your identity.

These lessons weren't taught explicitly but absorbed through years of observing the women around her—mothers, aunts, teachers—each fulfilling roles at the cost of their own aspirations.

Her life was a script written by others:

- **As a daughter,** she was expected to uphold the family's honor, often at the expense of her individuality.
- **As a wife,** she was supposed to bend, adapt, and fit herself into the mold of an "ideal partner."
- **As a member of society,** she was to smile through discomfort, comply with outdated norms, and never question authority.

Aradhana realizes that these roles, while seemingly noble, are prisons when imposed without consent.

The Generational Inheritance:

One of the most poignant realizations Aradhana has is that these expectations are not new. They are part of a generational cycle, passed down like an heirloom. Her grandmother, a woman who never had the chance to choose her own path, instilled in her mother the idea that sacrifice is the hallmark of a "good woman." Her mother, in turn, passed it down to her.

But now, Aradhana stands at a crossroads. She sees the generational burden for what it is—a legacy of compliance—and decides it ends with her.

Divine Parallels: Goddess Sita

Traditionally portrayed as the epitome of virtue and sacrifice, Sita's life was steeped in societal expectations. From her unquestioning loyalty to her exile in the forest, her story is often used to exemplify the ideal woman—patient, silent, and self-sacrificing.

However, this narrative overlooks Sita's strength. When Sita chooses to return to the Earth rather than continue proving her virtue, she makes a powerful statement. She refuses to be reduced to a symbol of compliance or a pawn in others' narratives. This act of reclamation is a radical assertion of her worth, showing that true strength lies not in enduring unreasonable expectations but in walking away from them.

Aradhana sees herself in Sita. Both women are misunderstood, labeled as defiant for choosing dignity over approval. Inspired by the Goddess, Aradhana begins to reframe her own story—not as one of rebellion, but of self-respect.

Aradhana's transformation begins with small, deliberate actions:

- **Setting boundaries**: She learns to say no to requests and obligations that drain her. It's uncomfortable at first, but each refusal strengthens her resolve.
- **Revisiting her dreams**: She pulls out an old sketchbook, a reminder of her love for art, and begins to draw again. It's a quiet rebellion against the years she spent suppressing her creativity.

- **Redefining relationships:** She starts honest conversations with her family, acknowledging their hurt but refusing to compromise her newfound freedom.

Reflection and Practical Insights:

1. What roles am I playing that don't align with my authentic self?
2. How have generational expectations shaped my identity?
3. What would it feel like to release the weight of others' dreams and honor my own?

Mantra:
"I release the weight of expectations. I choose to honor my truth."

CHAPTER THREE

EMBRACING THE WILDNESS WITHIN

"She was untamed, wild, and free—not in spite of her strength, but because of it."

The Fear of Being Too Much:

Aradhana has reached a turning point in her journey—she is no longer willing to shrink herself to fit the mold society has cast for her. Yet, as she steps into her power, she encounters a deep, underlying fear: the fear of being "too much." It's not just about how others perceive her; it's about the discomfort she feels within herself. She's afraid of being too bold, too loud, too ambitious, too passionate, too unapologetically herself. Growing up, she was taught that a "good woman" is quiet, obedient, and accepts the roles assigned to her without resistance. But now that she has tasted freedom, this fear is the only thing standing between her and the fullness of who she is meant to become.

One day, she remembers a piece of wisdom her grandmother shared with her: "A woman who speaks her mind will be called a witch. A woman who owns her body will be called impure. But the truth is, she is simply a woman who knows her power." This statement sparks a profound shift in Aradhana's heart. She realizes that her wildness—the refusal to conform—is not something to fear or suppress, but something to embrace and celebrate.

The Divine Feminine: Wild and Free

In this chapter, we explore the sacred power of the wild woman archetype, which aligns with the untamed essence of the Divine Feminine. The wild woman is not about chaos or destruction, but about living authentically and unapologetically. This is a force that cannot be bound by societal expectations. It is about standing tall in your truth, regardless of the judgments or labels others may place upon you.

One profound example of the wild woman is Goddess Durga. As a warrior goddess, Durga embodies both fierce strength and deep compassion. She fights not just for victory, but for truth and justice, balancing her primal power with a sense of protection and care for the world. Durga's wildness is not reckless—it is purposeful, channeling her strength to achieve balance. Aradhana's own defiance, as she embraces her power, mirrors Durga's fierce determination to live authentically, without compromise.

Aradhana's Transformation

Aradhana begins to realize that embracing her wildness is not just a path to personal freedom, but also a necessary step in reclaiming her whole self. As she sheds the societal labels that have stifled her, she taps into her creative, free-spirited energy. Her wardrobe shifts to reflect this new energy—bold, vibrant colors and patterns that mirror her spirit. Her hair, once neatly tied, now flows freely, a visual representation of the wildness she is learning to embrace within herself.

At work, Aradhana becomes more outspoken in meetings. She shares her ideas without hesitation, no longer consumed by the fear of rejection. Her trust in her own intuition and instincts grows stronger, and she no longer doubts her own worth or abilities. She is learning to speak her truth, even if it disrupts the comfort of others.

The Role of Anger in Reclaiming Power:

As Aradhana continues to grow into her full power, she must confront an emotion that has been suppressed for most of her life: anger. Society often teaches women to suppress their anger, to make it disappear beneath the surface, and to never let it show. But as she taps into her wildness, Aradhana learns that anger can be a powerful force for change, not something to be feared or ashamed of.

Anger, when channeled correctly, is not destructive—it's a fire that burns away what no longer serves us. For Aradhana, her anger becomes a catalyst for transformation. She is angry at the years of silence, at being diminished, at being told to conform. But rather than letting her anger consume her, she uses it to fuel her courage and boldness.

Connection to Divine Feminine: Goddess Parvati

We also get an inspiration from the story of Goddess Parvati, who exemplifies both gentleness and strength. Parvati's transformation from a gentle maiden to the fierce goddess who stands beside Lord Shiva reflects every woman's journey toward reclaiming her full power. Parvati's strength is not about fitting into a prescribed mold or imitating masculine power—it lies in her ability to honor both her softness and her fierce energy.

Like Parvati, Aradhana learns that her true power lies not in suppressing her wildness, but in integrating it fully into her being. She begins to see that her wildness, her refusal to conform, is the truest form of femininity—not something to be ashamed of, but something to embrace and honor.

Reflection and Practical Insights :

- **What does my "wildness" look like?**
- **What fears arise when I think about embracing my full self?**
- **How can I use anger as a tool for transformation?**

How to?

- **Reconnect with your wildness**: Begin to express yourself more authentically. This might mean dressing in a way that aligns with how you truly feel or speaking your mind in situations where you've stayed silent before. Start small, but aim for more regular acts of self-expression.
- **Challenge the fear of being "too much"**: When you feel the fear of being "too much," ask yourself: What is so wrong with being bold, passionate, or outspoken? Challenge the belief that you must shrink to fit others' expectations. The more you embrace your fullness, the more you will inspire others to do the same.
- **Use anger to propel forward**: If you find yourself angry or frustrated, don't suppress it. Acknowledge it, sit with it, and ask yourself what it's trying to tell you. Is it a sign that something needs to change? Use that energy to fuel your next step forward, whether in your career, relationships, or personal growth.
- **Honor both your gentleness and strength**: Just like Goddess Parvati, integrate both your soft and fierce aspects. Recognize that true power comes from embracing all parts of yourself—your compassion, your creativity, your strength, and your wildness.

Mantra:
"I embrace my wildness, for in it lies my strength."

CHAPTER FOUR

Defying Expectations, Redefining Respect

"Respect is not a favor; it's a foundation."

The Weight of Unspoken Rules

Aradhana has begun to reclaim her voice, to live in alignment with her truth. But one thing continues to weigh heavily on her—respect. It's a word often thrown around like a shield, a term used to manipulate and control behavior. For years, Aradhana has lived by the rules of respect as dictated by her family, society, and culture. It was always about submission, silence, and bending to the will of others.

At work, she's expected to keep her opinions in check, to laugh off inappropriate comments, to go along with the flow. At family gatherings, she's told to smile politely, to follow her mother's example of "perfect daughterhood," even if it means suppressing her dreams. Her husband expects her to always put the needs of the family first, without question, without protest.

The problem? These expectations are not rooted in mutual respect—they are demands for compliance, a call to play the part others have written for her.

Challenging the Concept of Respect

One night, while sitting with a friend over coffee, Aradhana hears a phrase that shakes her to her core: "Respect is not about silence; it's about honoring the truth of each person, including yourself."

This statement forces Aradhana to reconsider everything she thought she knew about respect. For too long, she has believed that respect means deferring to others, allowing their wants and needs to take precedence over her own. But in that moment, she realizes that true respect is not about holding her tongue or shrinking herself for the comfort of others. True respect is about the freedom to express herself honestly, to speak her truth, and to expect the same from others.

The Divine Feminine and Respect: The Story of Sita

Aradhana reflects on the story of Goddess Sita, a figure who is often held up as a symbol of grace, patience, and dignity. Sita's life, however, was marred by the expectations placed upon her by others, especially her husband, Lord Rama. Despite her unparallel loyalty, her strength, and her purity, Sita's character was constantly put to the test. After her rescue from Ravana's captivity, her purity was questioned by her own husband, forcing her to undergo the trial of fire—an act that became emblematic of the society's unwillingness to honor a woman's truth.

In the story of Sita, Aradhana sees an intense parallel to her own life. Sita becomes a tragic symbol of how women's respect is often contingent on their adherence to societal standards—standards that disregard their inherent worth, even when they have done nothing wrong. In Sita's case, her purity and worth were scrutinized, yet she was forced to undergo trials to prove herself. The expectation was not for her to be true to herself, but to fit into a mold created by society and by her husband's expectations.

However, what makes Sita's story powerful isn't just the burden she bore but her strength in the face of it. Sita's journey was one of immense personal dignity and quiet fortitude, even as she faced public humiliation and judgment. Her story demonstrates that respect should not be conditional or something that is earned by submission or sacrifice. True respect is inherent—it is not something that can be withdrawn based on another's judgment.

Aradhana relates to Sita's suffering, feeling the weight of expectations that demand she behave in a way that fits others' perceptions of what is "respectable." But she also sees in Sita the power of reclaiming one's dignity, of holding fast to one's self-worth, even when the world demands otherwise. Sita's story becomes a source of inspiration for Aradhana, as she realizes that respect should never come at the cost of one's identity, autonomy, or dignity.

Aradhana now understands that respecting herself means challenging the way respect has been demanded by society, family, and even her partner. She sees Sita as a figure who was forced to prove her respectability through trials, but who ultimately remained true to herself, even when it was the hardest thing to do.

The Struggle of Speaking Out:

When Aradhana confronts her husband about a recent decision he made without consulting her, she finds herself torn. He dismisses her feelings, saying, "You know this is how we do things. Why question it now?"

For a moment, Aradhana hesitates. Is she overreacting? Should she just let it go, as she has in the past? But then, she remembers what she learned about respect—that it's not about keeping quiet to maintain peace. It's about honoring her truth and the truth of the situation.

With newfound clarity, Aradhana asserts her feelings. She explains why the decision was not fair to her and how it made her feel disrespected. The conversation is difficult, and her husband responds defensively, but Aradhana stands firm. She doesn't shrink back, nor does she compromise on her boundaries.

The outcome? Not perfection, but progress. The conversation opens the door for deeper communication, and her husband, though uncomfortable, begins to recognize that Aradhana's need for respect is not a personal attack—it's a necessity for a healthy relationship.

Respect: A Two-Way Street

Aradhana now understands that true respect must be mutual. It is not something that one person simply gives to another—it must flow both ways. She starts to evaluate her relationships and the way respect has been given and received. Where has she been expected to swallow her feelings, her dreams, her desires? Where has she allowed others to define her worth?

In her friendships, she finds herself gravitating toward those who understand that respect isn't about silence or appeasing others. She seeks relationships where there is open dialogue, where mutual support is given and received, where boundaries are respected without question.

The Role of Boundaries in Respect

As Aradhana continues to grow, she learns the importance of setting healthy boundaries in her life. Boundaries are an essential part of self-respect—they define where she ends and others begin.

She sets boundaries with her family, explaining that while she loves them, she will no longer tolerate being dictated to or expected to conform to outdated expectations. She sets boundaries at work, ensuring that her time and energy are respected by colleagues. She establishes boundaries with her husband, articulating her need for a partnership based on equality, not dominance.

The more she sets these boundaries, the more empowered she feels. It becomes clear that respect is not a passive experience. It is an active process of continuously honoring herself and her needs while simultaneously respecting the needs of others.

Reflections and Practical Insights:

- **Where are you compromising your truth to maintain peace or meet expectations in your life?**
- **Are your relationships built on mutual respect, or do they involve one-sided demands?**
- **Where do you need to set clearer boundaries, and what steps can you take to enforce them?**
- **What would it look like to fully honor your voice in the most challenging areas of your life?**

How to?

- **Prioritize Self-Respect** :Reflect on areas where you feel undervalued and take small steps to assert your truth.
- **Set Clear Boundaries**: Identify situations where your boundaries are unclear or ignored, and communicate them firmly to protect your dignity.
- **Redefine Respect**: Challenge societal or cultural norms that equate respect with silence or submission. Embrace mutual respect rooted in equality and understanding.
- **Speak Up with Courage**: Practice expressing your needs and feelings, even in uncomfortable situations, to foster healthier relationships.
- **Seek Balanced Relationships**: Gravitate toward relationships where respect flows both ways and open communication is encouraged.

Mantra:
"I honor my truth and demand the respect that is my birthright."

CHAPTER FIVE

THE LIBERATION OF LETTING GO

"The moment you let go of the need to control, you open yourself up to a world of possibilities."

The Illusion of Control

Aradhana had spent her life trying to hold on. Hold on to expectations, hold on to relationships, hold on to a version of herself that she thought was acceptable to the world. She had controlled her narrative with precision, molding herself into the person she thought everyone else wanted her to be. But something was shifting inside her—a quiet, undeniable feeling that the more she held on, the more she was suffocating her true self.

One evening, as she scrolled through her phone, she stumbled upon a quote that stopped her cold: "The moment you let go of the need to control, you open yourself up to a world of possibilities." It was as if the universe had conspired to deliver this message at just the right time. Was this her sign to finally loosen her grip on the life she had meticulously constructed?

The Fear of Letting Go

But letting go wasn't easy. It felt like standing on the edge of a cliff, blindfolded, with no idea what lay beneath. Letting go of control meant abandoning the comfort of certainty, the familiar structure she had built to protect herself. What if she failed? What if, without her tight grip, everything fell apart?

Her thoughts spiraled as she pondered the idea of surrendering. How could she let go when so much of her identity had been built on control? How could she release the reins when there were so many things at stake? The thought of not being in charge felt terrifying.

But then Aradhana realized—wasn't it that fear of letting go that had been controlling her all along?

The Power of Surrender

Surrender wasn't about giving up or giving in. It wasn't about becoming passive or weak. It was about releasing the need for perfection, the need for control, the need to have everything go according to her plan. It was about trust—trusting herself, trusting life, and trusting the process.

One day, she took a small, brave step. At work, she allowed herself to let go of the overwhelming need to micromanage every detail of her project. She trusted her team, allowed them to take ownership, and watched as they thrived in ways she hadn't imagined. The world didn't collapse, her team didn't fail—it was as though a weight had lifted from her shoulders.

In that moment, Aradhana understood. Letting go was not the end of something; it was the beginning of something new. The space she created by releasing her need for control was filled with creativity, collaboration, and a sense of freedom she had never known before.

The Art of Non-Attachment

As Aradhana's journey of self-liberation continued, she

explored the concept of non-attachment—learning to be fully present in each moment without clinging to the outcome. She had always believed that her happiness depended on how things turned out, that she had to achieve specific goals to be worthy or fulfilled. But non-attachment taught her a powerful truth: happiness doesn't lie in the destination; it resides in the journey itself.

She began to apply this mindset to her relationships. Instead of clinging to the idea of how her marriage "should be," she allowed her connection with her husband to evolve naturally. Instead of holding him to expectations, she learned to embrace him for who he truly was, flaws and all, while also allowing herself to be seen and loved in her most authentic form. It wasn't always easy, and there were moments of discomfort, but slowly, the pressure lifted.

Aradhana realized that non-attachment didn't mean indifference. It didn't mean that she didn't care or that she was giving up. It simply meant that she was allowing space for life to unfold without forcing it into a specific mold. She was learning to be open, to flow with the current of life instead of fighting against it.

The Freedom of Letting Go

As Aradhana let go of her need for control, she began to experience a kind of freedom she had never known before. It wasn't the freedom she had once imagined—where everything would fall into place exactly as she had planned—but a deeper, more profound freedom. It was the freedom to be herself, to show up authentically in every aspect of her life.

At the same time, she noticed a shift in her energy. People around her seemed more drawn to her. She no longer felt the need to impress or to manage how others saw her. She became magnetic, not because she was trying, but because she was finally allowing herself to just be.

Her husband, too, felt this shift. He began to open up more, share more, and engage with her on a deeper level. There were no longer walls between them, only a shared understanding that they were in this together, learning and growing as individuals and as partners.

The Call to Adventure

One evening, Aradhana sat at her window, watching the sunset. She realized that the journey of letting go wasn't just about her relationships, her work, or her identity—it was about embracing life itself. There was a whole world out there, full of possibilities she had never even imagined, and she was ready to explore it.

Aradhana's story was far from over, but in that moment, she felt something shift inside her—a sense of excitement, of adventure. She was no longer trapped by the need for control. Instead, she was free to live fully, to take risks, and to trust that whatever came next would be just as it was meant to be.

The Next Step

As she closed her eyes and took a deep breath, she whispered to herself, "Let it go. Let it all go." The words felt like a mantra, an invitation to step into the unknown, to surrender fully to the adventure of life.

And in that surrender, Aradhana found the greatest freedom of all—the freedom to simply be.

Reflections and Practical Insights:

- Where are you trying to control outcomes, and how might letting go open up new possibilities?
- What fears come up when you think about surrendering control?
- How could embracing non-attachment help you experience more joy and freedom in your relationships?
- Where can you begin to embrace the adventure of life, free from the need to control every aspect?

How to?

- **Prioritize Surrender Over Control:** Reflect on where in your life you are holding on too tightly. Practice small acts of letting go—whether in your career, relationships, or personal goals—and trust the process.
- **Practice Non-Attachment:** Shift your focus from controlling outcomes to being present in the moment. Relinquish the need for specific results and allow life to unfold naturally.
- **Cultivate Trust in the Process :** Trust that things will work out even when they don't go as planned. Start by trusting those around you and letting go of the need to micromanage situations.
- **Explore New Possibilities:** Let go of rigid plans and embrace the uncertainty of life. Take risks, explore new opportunities, and trust that the journey itself holds valuable lessons.
- **Embrace the Freedom of Authenticity:** Take time to reflect on how you can be more authentic in your day-to-day interactions. Stop trying to conform and allow yourself to just be, experiencing life with more freedom

and joy.

Mantra:

"I release control and trust in the flow of life."

CHAPTER SIX

THE MIRROR OF FORGIVENESS

"Forgiveness is not a gift to them; it's liberation for yourself."

The Wound That Refused to Heal

Aradhana had always carried her pain like a badge of honor. Betrayals, disappointments, and unkind words from people she loved had etched themselves into her soul, forming a wall she thought was protecting her. In truth, the wall was keeping her trapped—isolated from peace, from love, and most importantly, from herself.

She would replay the moments of hurt in her mind like an old, scratched record. The harsh words her mother once said, the time her best friend walked away, the time her husband forgot a promise—each memory was a jagged shard of glass she held tightly, refusing to let go. Forgiveness, to her, had always felt like giving those who hurt her a free pass. Why should they get to move on unscathed while she bore the weight of their actions?

But as the years went by, the weight became too heavy to bear.

The Power of the Mirror

One evening, during a quiet moment of self-reflection, Aradhana sat in front of her mirror. It was something she rarely did—look at herself, really look. As her eyes met her own, she was startled by what she saw. There, in her reflection, was someone tired and burdened. Her pain had taken root in her body, her posture, her eyes.

It was then that she realized something profound: forgiveness wasn't about them. It was about her. Her inability to let go was not punishing those who had wronged her; it was punishing herself. The bitterness, the anger, the pain—it was all hers to carry, and it was hers to release.

Looking into the mirror, she said out loud, "I forgive you." At first, she didn't even know who the words were for. Her mother? Her friend? Her husband? Or maybe herself? The answer, she realized, was all of the above.

A Conversation with Her Inner Child

As Aradhana continued her journey of forgiveness, she decided to revisit her past. She found a photograph of herself as a child, one where she was laughing uncontrollably, her eyes sparkling with unfiltered joy. Where had that joy gone? What had dimmed her light?

In her mind, she imagined speaking to her younger self. "I'm sorry I let the world's harshness touch you," she said. "I'm sorry I didn't protect your joy." The conversation felt healing, as though she was mending a tear in her soul that had been there for years. She promised that little girl that she would start letting go—not for anyone else but for her, for the girl who once laughed freely.

The Challenge of Forgiving Others

Forgiving herself was one thing. Forgiving others? That was a battle. She started small—thinking of a friend who had hurt her feelings long ago. Did they even remember what they had done? Likely not. Holding on to that pain seemed absurd now, so she released it like a balloon into the sky.

Then came the bigger wounds. The family members who had criticized her, the friends who had abandoned her, the partner who had unknowingly taken her for granted. Each act of forgiveness was like pulling out a thorn embedded deep in her skin. It hurt, but it also brought relief.

When she finally forgave her husband for past hurts, it wasn't a grand gesture or a dramatic confrontation. It was a quiet decision she made in her heart. She chose to see him for who he was—a flawed human trying his best, just like her.

Forgiveness is a Process

Aradhana learned that forgiveness wasn't a one-time act. It was a process, sometimes a daily practice. Some days, the pain would resurface, and she'd have to remind herself of her decision to let go. And that was okay. Healing wasn't linear; it was messy and complicated, but it was worth it.

In forgiving others, she found herself becoming lighter, freer. The walls she had built around herself began to crumble, and in their place, she felt a sense of peace she hadn't known in years.

The Unexpected Gift

The most surprising part of Aradhana's journey was what forgiveness brought into her life. With each act of letting go, she found space for something new. New relationships, new opportunities, and most importantly, new love for herself.

Her marriage grew stronger as she stopped holding onto grudges. Her friendships deepened as she opened herself up to vulnerability. And in her quiet moments alone, she found a sense of contentment that was no longer tied to anyone else's actions.

The Mirror Again

One day, she returned to the mirror, the same one that had started her journey. This time, she smiled. The woman looking back at her was no longer burdened. She saw someone who had chosen to free herself, someone who had reclaimed her light.

"Thank you," she whispered to her reflection. And this time, she knew exactly who the words were for.

The Reflections and practical insights are that you put yourself in each aspect of this chapter and review.

Mantra:

"I forgive not because they deserve it, but because I do."

THE ART OF LOVING YOURSELF

"To love yourself is to give the world the gift of your whole being."

The Awakening

Aradhana had heard the phrase "love yourself" countless times before. It was the tagline of self-help books, the hashtag on Instagram posts, the refrain of well-meaning friends. But what did it really mean? It always sounded like a hollow platitude, a vague concept meant for people with spa appointments and endless free time.

For years, her idea of self-love had been transactional—a reward she gave herself after ticking off enough accomplishments on her to-do list. When she worked hard enough, looked good enough, or pleased enough people, she would allow herself a small indulgence: a new dress, a fancy dessert, a moment to breathe.

But true self-love? That felt like a luxury she couldn't afford.

Until the day she realized it wasn't.

A Love Letter to Herself

It started with a journal prompt: "If you could write a love letter to yourself, what would it say?" Aradhana hesitated. A love letter? To herself? The idea felt absurd, even indulgent. But something about the exercise intrigued her. She opened her journal and began to write:

"Dear Aradhana,

I see you. I see how hard you try, how much you care, and how deeply you feel. I see the strength in your struggles and the beauty in your imperfections. You are enough—today, tomorrow, and always."

As she wrote, something inside her shifted. For the first time, she wasn't seeking validation from others. She was giving it to herself. And it felt like coming home.

Reclaiming Her Body

One of the hardest parts of loving herself was reclaiming her relationship with her body. For years, Aradhana had viewed her body as a project—a never-ending work in progress. There was always something to fix, something to improve, something that wasn't good enough.

But as she stood in front of the mirror one morning, she decided to try something radical. Instead of criticizing herself, she whispered, "Thank you." Thank you to her legs for carrying her, to her arms for holding her loved ones, to her heart for beating tirelessly.

It wasn't easy. Some days, the old voices of self-doubt crept in, telling her she wasn't thin enough, pretty enough, or young enough. But on those days, she reminded herself: her worth wasn't tied to her appearance. Her body wasn't just something to look at—it was her home, her ally, her miracle.

The Ritual of Joy

Aradhana began incorporating small rituals of joy into her daily life. She bought herself flowers, not because it was a special occasion but because she deserved to be surrounded by beauty. She danced in her living room, not caring about how she looked, simply enjoying the rhythm of her movements. She spent time doing things that made her heart sing—painting, baking, walking barefoot on the grass.

These acts weren't about productivity or proving anything to anyone. They were about nourishing her soul, about giving herself permission to exist without justification.

Unlearning Conditional Love

One of the hardest lessons was unlearning the conditional love she had been taught. Throughout her life, she had internalized the message that love had to be earned—through achievements, sacrifices, or meeting others' expectations. But as she delved deeper into her journey, she realized that true love, especially for oneself, could never be conditional.

She no longer needed to be "perfect" to be worthy of love. She didn't need to please everyone, or do everything, or be everything. She was worthy simply because she existed.

The Ripple Effect

As Aradhana grew in her self-love, something surprising happened. Her relationships began to change. The more she respected and loved herself, the less she tolerated disrespect or indifference from others. She started setting boundaries—not out of anger or resentment, but out of love for herself.

At first, some people pushed back. They were used to the version of Aradhana who always said yes, who put everyone else's needs ahead of her own. But over time, those who truly valued her began to adapt. Her husband, in particular, noticed the change. "You seem...lighter," he said one evening. "Happier."

"I am," she replied with a smile. And for the first time, she meant it.

The Mirror of Love

One day, Aradhana returned to the mirror that had become a cornerstone of her journey. She looked at her reflection—not with judgment, but with tenderness. She saw a woman who had faced her fears, embraced her flaws, and chosen to love herself despite everything.

And in that moment, she knew: self-love wasn't a destination. It was a practice, a choice she would make every day. Some days would be easier than others, but she was committed to the journey. Because loving herself wasn't just about her—it was about the energy she brought into the world, the example she set for others, and the life she wanted to live.

The journey of loving yourself is neither linear nor quick. It is an ongoing practice that requires patience, compassion, and commitment. Aradhana's experience teaches us several key lessons:

Reflection and Practical Insights

- **Self-love is not a reward, it's a practice** – Love for oneself should not be earned through achievements or external validation. It's a daily choice, no matter how we feel about ourselves on a particular day.
- **Small acts of kindness matter** – Simple rituals like buying yourself flowers, dancing, or taking time for a hobby can serve as powerful reminders that you deserve joy without earning it.
- **Body acceptance is transformative** – Learning to appreciate and care for your body as it is, rather than constantly criticizing it, is a foundational aspect of self-love. True self-love isn't about perfection; it's about acceptance.
- **Boundaries are an act of self-love** – Setting healthy boundaries is not about being selfish but about protecting your well-being. When we respect ourselves, we teach others to respect us too.
- **Self-love ripples outward** – As we learn to love ourselves, we invite deeper connections with others and foster relationships based on mutual respect, kindness, and authenticity.
- **Embracing these practices**, Aradhana learned that self-love is not just an individual act—it is a gift to the world. And the more we give it to ourselves, the more we have to offer others.

Mantra:
"I am worthy of my own love, every single day."

CHAPTER EIGHT

THE COURAGE TO SAY NO

"No is a complete sentence."

The Burden of Yes

Aradhana had always been the "yes" person. Yes to extra work when her plate was already overflowing. Yes to family obligations that drained her spirit. Yes to friends who demanded her time without reciprocating the same energy. Saying yes felt easier, safer. It avoided conflict, made her likable, and kept the peace.

But it came at a cost. Every "yes" that went against her inner voice left her feeling depleted and resentful. Every time she agreed to something out of guilt or fear, she betrayed herself just a little more. And slowly, she began to realize that her constant acquiescence wasn't kindness—it was self-neglect.

The First No

The first time Aradhana said no, it felt like stepping into a storm. Her manager had asked her to stay late for the third time that week, a pattern she'd reluctantly accepted in the past. But this time, something shifted.

"No, I can't tonight. I've already made plans," she said, her voice steady but her heart racing.

Her manager's eyebrows shot up in surprise. "Plans? Can't they wait? This is important."

For a moment, Aradhana hesitated. The old script in her head urged her to backpedal, to apologize, to reconsider. But she didn't. "I understand, but I can't stay late tonight," she repeated firmly.

The conversation ended awkwardly, and Aradhana spent the rest of the evening questioning herself. But later, as she enjoyed a quiet dinner with a book she'd been meaning to read, she felt an unfamiliar sensation: freedom.

Redefining Boundaries

Saying no wasn't just about refusing demands; it was about creating space for herself. Aradhana began to think of her boundaries as invisible fences—flexible but firm, designed to protect her energy and peace.

At home, she stopped answering phone calls during her dedicated "me time." At work, she made it clear she wouldn't respond to emails after hours. In her relationships, she started noticing when her "yes" was driven by guilt rather than genuine desire. The more she honored her boundaries, the more empowered she felt.

Of course, not everyone reacted well. Some colleagues saw her newfound assertiveness as arrogance. Her mother remarked, "You've changed," with a hint of disapproval. But Aradhana understood now that "no" wasn't just a rejection; it was a declaration of her priorities.

The Challenge of Guilt

The hardest part of saying no wasn't the reaction of others—it was the guilt that followed. Aradhana had been conditioned to equate self-sacrifice with love, and every no felt like she was letting someone down.

To navigate this, she leaned into a mantra she had recently learned: "You can't pour from an empty cup." If she continued to overextend herself, she would have nothing left to give—not to her work, her family, or her passions. Every no she said was, in fact, a yes to herself.

Lessons from Nature

On a quiet weekend retreat, Aradhana found herself sitting by a stream, watching the water flow around rocks and fallen branches. The stream didn't apologize for changing direction. It didn't try to accommodate every obstacle in its path. It flowed naturally, effortlessly, adapting as needed.

In that moment, Aradhana realized that her journey wasn't about rigidly protecting herself from the world. It was about learning to flow, to choose her path without guilt or apology. Saying no wasn't resistance; it was alignment.

When No Becomes Yes

Interestingly, the more Aradhana practiced saying no, the more meaningful her yes became. She found herself saying yes to the things that truly mattered—yes to a late-night conversation with a friend who needed her, yes to an impromptu road trip that nourished her soul, yes to her dreams of pursuing a long-forgotten hobby.

Her life didn't feel smaller because of her boundaries; it felt richer, more intentional.

Reflection and Practical Insights:

- **Reflect on Your Automatic Yes:** Take a moment to think about the last time you said yes when you really wanted to say no. What was driving your response? Fear of conflict? Guilt? A desire to be seen as helpful? Understanding the "why" behind your yes is the first step to reclaiming your boundaries.
- **Redefine What No Means:** Saying no doesn't make you selfish or unkind. It's a way to protect your energy and prioritize what truly matters to you. A no to others is often a yes to yourself.
- **Practice Small Nos:** If saying no feels intimidating, start small. Say no to a minor request, like running an errand that someone could do themselves. Gradually build your confidence for bigger boundaries.
- **Set Clear Boundaries:** Use language that is respectful but firm. For example:

1. "I'm not available right now, but I can help tomorrow."
2. "That doesn't align with my priorities right now."
3. "Thank you for thinking of me, but I'll have to pass."

- **Overcome the Guilt:** Remember, guilt is a natural response when you start setting boundaries, especially if you're used to overgiving. Reframe guilt as a sign that you're prioritizing your well-being.
- **Celebrate Your Wins:** Each time you honor your boundaries, celebrate it as a victory. It's a step toward living authentically and empowering yourself.

Mantra:
"Every no I say is a yes to my well-being."

CHAPTER NINE

The Power of Letting Go

"Let go, or be dragged."

The Weight of Holding On

Aradhana had always been a person who held on tightly. She held on to relationships, even when they no longer served her. She held on to jobs that didn't make her happy. She held on to old beliefs, even when they kept her stuck. Letting go had always felt like a failure, like giving up, like admitting defeat. But the more she held on, the more she realized she was carrying a weight that was draining her energy and clouding her judgment.

Her hands were full, and yet, nothing truly nourished her.

The First Step Toward Release

The first time Aradhana consciously let go, she felt a profound sense of loss. It was a friendship she'd held on to out of loyalty, even though it had become toxic. There had been too many broken promises, too many disappointments. But the hardest part wasn't the decision itself—it was the aftermath.

She felt the emptiness of the space left behind, as though she had lost a part of herself. The absence of that friendship echoed in her heart. But as time passed, she began to feel something else—a sense of relief. The constant tug-of-war for attention, validation, and effort had stopped. She was free.

For the first time in years, Aradhana felt like she could breathe, like there was room for something better to come into her life.

The Fear of Letting Go

Letting go had always been tied to fear. What if she let go and never found something better? What if the void left behind was too much to bear?

Aradhana had long struggled with the fear of being alone, of failing, of not measuring up. But she began to realize that the fear of staying stuck was greater than the fear of letting go. She had been so focused on what she might lose that she couldn't see what she might gain.

Letting go didn't mean giving up—it meant making space for new possibilities, new growth, and new opportunities. It was about trusting that the universe had something better in store for her, something more aligned with her true self.

The Courage to Release

One evening, as she sat by the window, Aradhana thought about all the things she had been holding on to—old habits, outdated expectations, unresolved grudges, and dreams that no longer lit her soul on fire.

She realized that in order to step into the next phase of her life, she had to release the past. She had to let go of what no longer served her, no matter how attached she had become.

It was a quiet, powerful moment. She whispered to herself, "I release what no longer serves me." It wasn't just a phrase—it was a declaration.

The next day, she started by letting go of the small things—the habits that drained her, the clutter that filled her home. But it didn't stop there. Slowly, she began to let go of the bigger things—the limiting beliefs, the toxic relationships, the fears that had been keeping her stuck. Each release felt like shedding a layer of armor she no longer needed.

The more she let go, the lighter she became.

The Freedom of Letting Go

Aradhana soon discovered that letting go was not a loss—it was a liberation. By releasing the things that had weighed her down, she created space for joy, for clarity, and for new opportunities. She had room to grow, to expand, to embrace the unknown.

Letting go didn't mean she was abandoning her past—it meant she was choosing her future. It meant trusting that the people, experiences, and opportunities that were meant for her would find their way into her life.

And in letting go, she discovered something even more powerful: she could trust herself. She had the strength to face whatever came next, knowing that she had the courage to release what wasn't meant for her and embrace what was.

Releasing Expectations

One of the hardest things Aradhana had to let go of was her expectations. She had spent so much of her life trying to control the outcomes, trying to shape everything to her liking. But she realized that the more she held on to her expectations, the more she closed herself off to the beauty of life as it was.

When she stopped expecting things to go a certain way, when she let go of the need for control, she found that life unfolded in its own beautiful, unexpected ways.

Sometimes, the universe had a better plan for her than she could have imagined. By releasing her tight grip on what she thought should happen, she allowed herself to flow with life, to be open to new possibilities.

The Healing Power of Letting Go

Letting go was not just about creating space in her life—it was about healing. Aradhana had held on to old hurts for too long, allowing resentment and pain to fester. But with each release, she began to heal.

She forgave herself for the mistakes she had made. She forgave others for the hurts they had caused. She forgave life for not turning out the way she had imagined.

In forgiving, Aradhana experienced freedom. The burden of past regrets, the weight of old wounds, began to dissipate. She felt lighter, more at peace, and more connected to her true self.

Letting go was the key to her healing—it was the gateway to her peace.

Reflection and Practical Insights

- **Identify What You're Holding On To and How it helps you?** Take a moment to reflect on the things you've been holding on to. Is it a relationship, a job, a belief, or a habit? What is it costing you to hold on? Identifying what you're holding on to is the first step in freeing yourself from it.
- **Release What No Longer Serves You :** Start with small releases. Let go of physical clutter, negative self-talk, or habits that drain your energy. Over time, release bigger things—unhealthy relationships, outdated goals, and limiting beliefs. Trust that releasing will make space for something better.
- **Embrace the Freedom of Letting Go:** Letting go isn't about losing something—it's about gaining everything you need. Trust the process and embrace the freedom that comes with it. Let go of the need to control and allow life to unfold naturally.
- **Practice Forgiveness:** Forgiveness is an essential part of letting go. Forgive yourself for past mistakes, forgive others for their wrongs, and forgive life for not always going as planned. Forgiveness frees you from the past and opens you up to healing.

Mantra
"I release what no longer serves me, and in doing so, I make space for the life I am meant to live."

CHAPTER TEN

EMBRACING CHANGE

"Change is the only constant in life." — Heraclitus

The Resistance to Change

Aradhana had always been someone who liked stability. She liked routines, predictability, and knowing exactly what to expect from each day. Change felt like a disruption, an intrusion into her carefully curated world. She had always been resistant to it, fearing that it would throw her off balance and lead to something unknown or uncomfortable.

But, as she was beginning to understand, change wasn't something to fear. It was something to embrace. The more she resisted it, the more it seemed to challenge her, throwing her into situations that forced her to adapt. And yet, deep inside, she knew that change was not an enemy—it was an invitation to grow.

The Catalyst for Change

It wasn't until Aradhana found herself at a crossroads in her life that she realized change was inevitable. She had spent years in a job that no longer fulfilled her, stuck in a routine that offered no excitement. Relationships, too, had become stagnant, and her personal growth had plateaued.

One day, she stood still, looking at her reflection in the mirror. The face that stared back at her seemed familiar, yet distant. It was as if she had been sleepwalking through life, clinging to the security of her comfort zone, avoiding the discomfort of change.

That moment was her catalyst. Aradhana made the conscious decision to step into the unknown. She could no longer ignore the nagging feeling that there was something more—something beyond the life she had created. It was time to let go of the safety net and embrace change.

Facing the Fear of the Unknown

The fear of the unknown was one of the biggest obstacles Aradhana had to overcome. It was easier to stay in the familiar, even if it wasn't satisfying, than to face the uncertainty that change brought. But Aradhana began to realize that the fear of what could happen was often worse than the actual change itself.

She found that once she began to take small steps outside her comfort zone, the fear began to dissipate. She realized that she had the strength to face whatever came her way, even if she didn't know the exact outcome.

The unknown was not a void; it was a field of endless possibilities. Change, Aradhana learned, wasn't about losing control—it was about gaining freedom, flexibility, and the courage to explore what life had to offer.

The Growth That Comes with Change

Once Aradhana opened herself to the idea of change, she began to experience a growth she hadn't known before. She started pursuing new hobbies, trying out new skills, and saying yes to experiences that once scared her.

She felt more alive than she had in years. Change had sparked a renewed sense of curiosity and excitement in her.

She started taking risks, trusting that even if things didn't work out as planned, she would be able to handle it.

This growth wasn't always linear. There were moments of doubt, fear, and setbacks. But Aradhana now understood that growth was a process, not a destination. It wasn't about achieving perfection—it was about evolving, learning, and becoming the best version of herself.

Letting Go of Perfection

In her pursuit of change, Aradhana realized that she had been holding herself to an impossible standard. She had been trying to control every outcome, fix every flaw, and perfect every aspect of her life. But perfection, she learned, was an illusion.

Letting go of the need to be perfect was liberating. It allowed her to be more authentic, more spontaneous, and more forgiving of herself. She no longer viewed mistakes as failures but as valuable lessons in her journey of growth.

Perfectionism had kept her stuck in fear. But once she embraced the idea that she was enough just as she was, imperfections and all, change became easier to navigate. She began to appreciate the messiness of life—the unpredictable twists, the surprises, and the lessons that came with it.

Embracing the Present Moment

Change, Aradhana discovered, had the unique ability to bring her into the present moment. When everything around her was shifting, she couldn't help but be fully present. There was no room for distractions or worries about the future.

She learned to focus on the now, appreciating the small victories, the simple moments, and the beauty of her journey. The more she embraced the present, the more she realized that change wasn't something that happened to her—it was something that was happening within her, every single day.

Embracing change allowed her to align with the flow of life, trusting that every moment was leading her to exactly where she needed to be.

The Gifts of Change

As Aradhana continued to navigate the changes in her life, she began to see the gifts it brought. Change had brought her clarity, resilience, and a deeper understanding of herself. It had taught her the value of flexibility and adaptation, and most importantly, it had shown her that she was capable of handling whatever came her way.

The greatest gift of change, however, was the realization that life was never stagnant. It was always in motion, always evolving. By embracing change, Aradhana was no longer waiting for life to happen to her—she was actively creating it.

Reflection and Practical Insights:

- **Recognize the Resistance** :Take a moment to reflect on the areas of your life where you're resisting change. What are you afraid of? What are you holding on to? Identifying your resistance is the first step toward embracing the unknown.
- **Take Small Steps** :Embrace change by taking small steps. Start by making one change in your routine, trying something new, or challenging a belief that no longer serves you. Over time, these small changes will build momentum.
- **Let Go of Perfection**: Release the need for perfection. Understand that change is messy, and growth happens through trial, error, and resilience. Be kind to yourself as you navigate the uncertainties.
- **Stay Present** :In times of change, focus on the present moment. Trust that everything is unfolding as it should. Celebrate small wins and appreciate where you are, knowing that each step brings you closer to the person you're becoming.

Mantra
"Change is the canvas of my life; each stroke is an opportunity to grow, evolve, and embrace the unknown."

CHAPTER ELEVEN

THE POWER OF SELF-COMPASSION

"Be kind to yourself; you're doing the best you can."

The Struggle with Self-Criticism

Aradhana had always been her own harshest critic. If she made a mistake, no matter how small, she would replay it in her mind over and over again. She held herself to impossibly high standards, expecting perfection in everything she did. This constant self-criticism was exhausting and left her feeling unworthy of her own love and respect.

Every time she stumbled, she berated herself, thinking she should have done better. This mindset wasn't just limiting—it was suffocating. It prevented her from embracing her achievements and learning from her mistakes. And, more than anything, it kept her from being kind to herself.

A Shift in Perspective

It wasn't until Aradhana stumbled upon a conversation about self-compassion that things began to change. A friend, during a casual chat, mentioned how she had learned to speak kindly to herself in moments of struggle.

"Self-compassion is not about being complacent or excusing your mistakes," her friend explained. "It's about accepting your humanity, acknowledging your imperfections, and treating yourself with the same kindness you'd offer to a friend who's going through a tough time."

That idea struck a chord with Aradhana. She had always been generous with others, extending patience, kindness, and understanding. But when it came to herself, she was unforgiving. Why hadn't she been showing up for herself in the same way?

The Practice of Self-Compassion

The first step toward self-compassion was simple but profound: being mindful of how she spoke to herself. Aradhana began noticing the harsh inner dialogue she carried. Instead of thinking, "You should've done better," she started replacing it with, "You did your best, and that's enough."

Whenever she encountered a setback, she gently reminded herself that mistakes were a part of growth. "I'm allowed to make mistakes. I'm allowed to be human," she would tell herself.

Instead of spiraling into negative self-judgment, Aradhana began to treat herself as she would a close friend. When she felt overwhelmed or exhausted, she allowed herself rest without guilt. When she felt insecure, she practiced self-soothing, reminding herself of her strengths.

Incorporating this practice wasn't easy—it felt strange at first. But over time, Aradhana noticed a shift. She began to feel lighter, more at ease with herself. She realized that self-compassion wasn't about perfection; it was about acceptance.

The Inner Voice of Kindness

One evening, after an especially challenging day at work, Aradhana found herself in her living room, feeling completely drained. Her mind raced with thoughts of all the things she hadn't accomplished. The inner critic was loud and unforgiving, telling her she hadn't done enough.

But then, she paused. She closed her eyes, took a deep breath, and let her heart lead.

Instead of engaging with the critical voice, she began to speak kindly to herself. "You've been working hard. It's okay to not be perfect. You're doing the best you can, and that's enough for today."

For the first time in a long while, she felt a sense of peace wash over her. The self-criticism faded, replaced by a deep sense of compassion and understanding.

Releasing the Need for Approval

Part of Aradhana's struggle with self-compassion stemmed from her constant need for external validation. She had spent so much time seeking approval from others—whether it was from her boss, her family, or her friends. She believed that only through their acknowledgment could she feel worthy.

But as she began practicing self-compassion, she realized that true worth didn't depend on the approval of others. It came from within.

She no longer needed to chase validation. She began to trust that her efforts, even if unnoticed by others, were valuable. She found comfort in knowing that she didn't have to prove anything to anyone. She was worthy because she existed, because she tried, because she was learning and growing every day.

The Role of Self-Compassion in Healing

Self-compassion also played a key role in Aradhana's healing journey. There had been wounds in her past—moments where she had felt rejected, hurt, or abandoned. At first, these wounds had seemed impossible to heal. But when she started showing herself compassion, she noticed that healing became possible.

Instead of pushing away the pain or ignoring it, she began to approach it with kindness. She allowed herself to grieve, to feel, and to process the emotions without judgment.

In doing so, she discovered that healing wasn't about erasing the past; it was about accepting it, embracing the lessons it had taught her, and moving forward with love and understanding for herself.

The Freedom of Self-Love

As Aradhana continued to cultivate self-compassion, she found herself becoming more liberated. She no longer felt the weight of self-criticism or the need to constantly prove herself. She was free to make mistakes without shame, to pursue her dreams without fear of failure, and to live in the present moment with an open heart.

Self-compassion became the foundation of her life. It gave her the strength to take risks, the courage to be authentic, and the grace to navigate challenges with patience and love. She understood now that she didn't have to be perfect to be worthy of love, happiness, and success.

Reflection and Practical Insights:

- **Observe Your Inner Dialogue:** Pay attention to how you speak to yourself. Are you kind or critical? If you notice negative self-talk, practice replacing it with affirming and compassionate thoughts.
- **Practice Self-Soothing:** When you're feeling overwhelmed or stressed, use self-soothing techniques. This could include deep breathing, positive affirmations, or simply taking a moment to rest.
- **Allow Yourself Imperfection:** Understand that mistakes and setbacks are part of the human experience. You are allowed to make them without judgment. Allow yourself grace as you grow and evolve.
- **Celebrate Your Progress:** Every step forward, no matter how small, is worth celebrating. Acknowledge your achievements and progress, and treat yourself with the same kindness you would offer a loved one.
- **Trust Your Worth :**Your worth is not determined by external approval or perfection. It comes from within. Trust that you are valuable simply because you are you.

Mantra:
"I am deserving of love and kindness, especially from myself."

CHAPTER TWELVE

Embracing Imperfection: The Art of Letting Go

"Perfection is not attainable, but if we chase perfection, we can catch excellence." — Vince Lombardi

The Fast-Paced Race to Nowhere

Aradhana had been living life in the fast lane for as long as she could remember. Every morning felt like a sprint, checking off a never-ending to-do list, racing against the clock, and striving to make everything perfect. Her inbox was flooded, her calendar booked, her thoughts scattered. It was a blur of achievements, goals, and metrics—all wrapped in the pursuit of perfection.

She wasn't alone in this. Around her, people ran similar races—always hustling, always aiming for something more, faster, better. The world had evolved into a place where everything had to be immediate—emails answered in seconds, success stories overnight, beauty "perfected" with filters, and social media snapshots showing only the highlights, never the struggle.

But despite the speed, Aradhana often felt like she was running in place. Every time she checked off a box, another one appeared. Every time she accomplished something, the bar was raised higher. Her pursuit of perfection, it seemed, had become a cycle of endless striving—and yet, she never quite arrived at where she thought she would.

The Trap of Perfectionism

She realized that the drive for perfection wasn't just about achieving the ideal end result. It was rooted in an unspoken belief: that perfection meant validation, that a flawless outcome would finally prove she was enough.

Perfectionism was a subtle, insidious force. It promised satisfaction but delivered only exhaustion. The more she chased it, the further it slipped away, like trying to grab smoke with bare hands. But worse than the exhaustion was the emptiness. Achievements that once felt significant now felt hollow, the momentary satisfaction replaced by a hunger for the next, bigger thing.

She wasn't just perfectionistic about her work—Aradhana had applied the same mindset to her personal life. She expected flawless relationships, perfect self-image, and well-curated experiences. When things didn't fit the picture-perfect mold, she felt like a failure. It was exhausting, and in the rare moments when she didn't meet her own impossibly high standards, she'd drown in a sea of guilt.

The Identity of Perfection

The truth that Aradhana had long avoided came crashing down: she was operating from the identity of perfection. The desire for flawless outcomes had become so ingrained in her that she began to think that perfection was part of who she was. But as the facade cracked, she saw something startling. Perfection wasn't her identity. It was an armor she had worn to shield herself from vulnerability, from failure, from judgment.

Without that armor, who was she? A person who had made mistakes, who had grown through pain, who wasn't always on top of her game. And that was okay. In fact, it was more than okay—it was human. She had been so focused on becoming perfect that she had missed the beauty in being beautifully imperfect.

The Fear of Letting Go

Letting go of the need for perfection wasn't easy. Aradhana had been taught that in a world that rewarded speed, productivity, and flawless output, failure was something to be feared. She had spent so long operating on the assumption that perfection was the only acceptable outcome that imperfection seemed like an alien concept.

But what if imperfection was the key to freedom? What if failure wasn't the end, but a necessary part of the process? What if, just maybe, slowing down and accepting the imperfections of life could lead to something greater than perfection ever promised?

The New Pace: Slowing Down to Speed Up

One day, Aradhana stopped. She didn't cancel her meetings, drop her projects, or resign from her responsibilities. Instead, she slowed down—in her mind, in her heart, in the way she interacted with the world.

What she found was astonishing. By letting go of perfection and embracing the unpredictability of life, she didn't become less efficient. She became more aligned with herself. Her work didn't suffer. In fact, it flourished, because she wasn't holding herself to impossible standards. She allowed her ideas to flow without the constraint of expecting immediate perfection.

It was like driving with the brakes on and suddenly letting go. The car didn't lose speed. It found its speed, gliding effortlessly. This was the magic of slowing down. In accepting that things could—and often should—be imperfect, Aradhana discovered that life didn't have to be a race. It could be a journey.

What she realized, as she embraced the messy, unpredictable flow of life, was that she wasn't trying to reach a destination. She was living the journey itself.

The Art of Imperfection: Letting Go of Control

Aradhana started to redefine what success meant for her. Success wasn't a perfect outcome—it was growth, learning, and progress. It was about being present in the process, not just obsessing over the destination.

She began to appreciate the beauty of things that were imperfect—her work, her relationships, her moments of spontaneity. She stopped clinging to an idealized version of herself and allowed herself to make mistakes. When she did, she didn't spiral into guilt. Instead, she paused, reflected, and learned.

She found joy in the unplanned, in the unexpected. She realized that the best moments were often the ones that didn't go according to plan. And when things did fall apart, she no longer saw it as a failure, but as a part of the ebb and flow of life, something that made the story richer.

The Collective Obsession with Perfection

As Aradhana looked around, she noticed that she wasn't the only one caught in this perfectionist trap. Everywhere she looked, there were people constantly chasing an ideal. The world, it seemed, had bought into the myth that the only way to succeed was to be perfect.

But in the process of trying to keep up with this fast-paced, idealized version of life, everyone was losing something—self-acceptance, joy, and most of all, the ability to live rather than just achieve.

The culture of perfectionism that had infiltrated her life and the lives of those around her was a carefully constructed illusion. It kept people moving faster, achieving more, but ultimately left them unfulfilled.

The Truth About Perfectionism

Aradhana understood now that the chase for perfection had little to do with who she truly was. Perfection wasn't about flawless outcomes; it was about embracing the imperfections in the process, learning from them, and moving forward without judgment.

The real secret wasn't about getting everything right. It was about letting go of the need to be right. It was about accepting that the messiness, the failures, and the mistakes were just as valuable as the successes.

In fact, they were often the most important part of the journey.

A New Mantra: Progress, Not Perfection

With this new understanding, Aradhana made a vow to herself: she would no longer chase perfection. Instead, she would embrace progress—the small steps forward, the growth in every mistake, the lessons learned along the way. She would let go of the race and start walking at her own pace, embracing the imperfections as they came.

And as she did, something unexpected happened. Her life became richer. Her relationships became deeper. Her work became more fulfilling. By giving herself permission to be imperfect, she found the freedom to truly live—unhindered by the illusion of perfection, and fully engaged with the beauty of life, as it was.

Reflection and Practical Insights:

- **Embrace Your Flaws**: What would happen if you stopped trying to hide your imperfections and instead embraced them? Could they become the source of your strength?
- **Let Go of the Race**: Reflect on areas of your life where you've been running too fast. What would it feel like to slow down and allow things to unfold naturally?
- **Challenge Perfectionism: Ask yourself:** Why do I feel the need for perfection? What would it look like if I let go of this expectation?
- **Celebrate the Journey**: Focus less on the outcome and more on the process. Celebrate the progress, not the perfection.
- **Create Space for Imperfection**: Give yourself and others permission to be imperfect. See what happens when you stop striving for flawless outcomes and instead start appreciating the journey.

Mantra:
"Perfection is a myth. Progress is the truth."

CHAPTER THIRTEEN

THE SACRED AND THE UNTAMED

"In embracing both the sacred and the untamed within us, we become whole."

The Awakening of the Sacred

For most of her life, Aradhana had defined herself by the roles she played—dutiful daughter, devoted wife, and dedicated mother. She had always been the anchor, the one who ensured everything ran smoothly, whether it was at work, at home, or in her relationships. Her identity was deeply tied to being "everything to everyone," to the sacred roles she embodied. She was the giver, the caretaker, the nurturer—the one others could rely on. But in this quest for perfection and service, she lost sight of herself. The sacred self she had come to worship slowly began to fade, swallowed by the relentless weight of expectations, self-neglect, and perfectionism.

But beneath this quiet sacrifice, there was always another part of her. The untamed, fiery force that longed for freedom, imperfection, and authenticity. It was the side of Aradhana that resisted the boxes she had been forced into, the one that yearned for liberation from the flawless image she was expected to maintain. As Aradhana entered midlife, this untamed voice grew louder, demanding that she rediscover herself, shedding the layers of perfect motherhood, perfect marriage, and the expectations placed on her by her parents.

Reconnecting with the Untamed: The Mother's Rebellion

The turning point came when Aradhana realized that motherhood was not just about checklists and responsibilities. It wasn't only about making sure her children were fed, clothed, and emotionally nurtured. Motherhood, for Aradhana, was about showing her children that it was okay to be imperfect. It was about teaching them that love, joy, and connection didn't rely on perfection. For so long, she had tried to be the perfect mother, the one who always had everything under control, but it became clear that this version of motherhood wasn't sustainable.

She allowed herself to be vulnerable in front of her children. She showed them that she, too, could be tired, confused, and human. She no longer felt the need to have all the answers. This was the shift—the moment Aradhana began to let go of perfection. In doing so, not only was she liberating herself, but she was also teaching her children a vital lesson: they didn't have to be perfect to be loved. Through her vulnerability, she showed them the beauty of embracing imperfection.

Her relationship with her children blossomed in this newfound freedom. She started to trust them more, allowing them to make mistakes, to discover their own way. She stopped trying to control their every move and, instead, began to guide them with love and respect. This shift in her parenting freed her, just as it empowered her children to trust their instincts and grow into their own untamed selves.

The Dance with Her Parents: Breaking the Cycle

Aradhana's journey of liberation also extended to her relationship with her parents. Growing up, she had always sought to please them, to meet their standards of success, responsibility, and perfection. But as she entered midlife, she began to realize how much of her life had been shaped by their expectations. She had lived as the dutiful daughter, fulfilling their vision for her, and in doing so, had lost touch with her own desires, dreams, and voice.

It was time for Aradhana to break the cycle. She started having real, honest conversations with her parents—not just about her responsibilities but about who she was becoming as an individual. For the first time, she allowed herself to be vulnerable with them, to express her own needs, desires, and dreams for the future. These conversations were difficult but transformative. She no longer felt the need for their approval to validate her worth.

Her parents, too, began to see her differently. They realized that their daughter was no longer the perfect image they had envisioned. She was a complex, multidimensional woman with her own struggles and aspirations. Slowly, the dynamic between them shifted. Their relationship evolved from one of obligation to one of mutual respect and understanding, as Aradhana embraced her autonomy and their relationship became more authentic.

Parenting with Freedom: The Sacred Imperfection

As Aradhana liberated herself in her motherhood, she also understood that she couldn't fully give to her children what she didn't give herself: the freedom to be untamed and imperfect. She began to carve out time for herself without guilt. It was not a rejection of her children, but a necessary reclamation of her own identity. She needed to prioritize her own needs, passions, and dreams in order to show her children that it was okay to do the same.

Aradhana started to take weekends away, to engage in activities that had nothing to do with being a mother or wife. She took time to explore her own hobbies, her desires, and her creative self. In doing so, she taught her children an invaluable lesson: that self-care was essential, that honoring one's boundaries wasn't selfish, and that a balanced life required nourishing both your responsibilities and your personal desires.

Her relationship with her children evolved further. No longer the sole caretaker and controller, Aradhana became a guide, encouraging them to explore their own identities, to make mistakes, and to find their own path. She stopped trying to mold them into a version of herself or the world she envisioned. Instead, she allowed them the freedom to embrace their untamed selves.

A New Relationship with Her Partner

Aradhana's journey of liberation also transformed her marriage. For years, she had tried to be the ideal wife—the one who never complained, the one who always knew how to keep things running smoothly, the one who always put her husband's needs before her own. But as she embraced her untamed self, she realized that this wasn't sustainable. A marriage built on perfectionism was suffocating.

She began to have open and honest conversations with her husband about her own needs, desires, and the importance of both partners finding freedom within the relationship. They talked about the roles they had been playing for years—the roles that had limited their growth and stifled their individual selves. Together, they started shedding the expectations of who they were "supposed" to be. They allowed their relationship to become more fluid, more authentic. The bond deepened as they both embraced the untamed aspects of themselves, recognizing that it was only in embracing their full selves—flaws and all—that they could truly grow together.

The Sacred and the Untamed: A Balanced Dance

Aradhana's journey wasn't about choosing between the sacred and the untamed—it was about learning to let both coexist. The sacred roles of motherhood, marriage, and career could exist alongside the untamed need for freedom, creativity, and self-expression. She learned that both were essential to her well-being.

The sacred was found in the quiet moments of connection and nurturing, in the love she gave to her family and work. The untamed was in the spontaneous moments of joy, in embracing imperfection, in living freely and authentically. Aradhana realized that her life didn't need to be defined by perfectionism; it was defined by her authenticity, her willingness to live in alignment with both her responsibilities and her wild, untamed desires.

In the dance between the sacred and the untamed, Aradhana found her true freedom. She was no longer bound by the need for perfection. She had liberated herself from the confines of expectation and embraced the expansiveness of living authentically. She had found peace in the tension between these two parts of herself, allowing them to coexist in harmony.

Reflection and Practical Insights

- **Liberating Your Parenting**: Let go of the idea of being the perfect parent. Embrace the chaos and imperfections of parenthood. Allow your children to see you as human, as someone who has dreams and desires of your own. Teach them that love, connection, and joy don't require perfection.

- **Reclaiming Your Relationship with Your Parents**: Have honest conversations with your parents about who you are and what you need. Let go of the idea of being the perfect child. Embrace the complexity of your relationship and create space for mutual respect and understanding.

- **Living Authentically in Relationships**: Whether with your children, partner, or family, allow yourself the freedom to be imperfect. Embrace the untamed parts of yourself and share them with those you love. Your authenticity will strengthen your relationships.

- **Prioritizing Yourself Without Guilt**: Remember, you can be sacred to others and untamed for yourself. Make space for your own needs, passions, and freedom. Honor your boundaries and allow yourself to step into your untamed self.

Mantra:
"In embracing both the sacred and the untamed within me, I create a life that is whole, authentic, and free."

CHAPTER FOURTEEN

THE DANCE OF FREEDOM

Aradhana stood at the edge of a new beginning, gazing out at the horizon. The sun, just beginning to set, bathed the sky in hues of gold and pink, as if the world itself were honoring the transformation she had undergone. Her life no longer felt like a series of isolated moments; it felt like an unfolding symphony, each note more aligned with who she truly was.

The Sacred and the Untamed had always lived within her, hidden beneath layers of expectation, fear, and obligation. But now, she was both of them. The sacred was no longer a distant concept, something lofty and untouchable. It was woven into her daily rhythms, her breath, the quiet moments of reflection, and the spontaneous bursts of joy. The untamed was no longer a chaotic force to be tamed, but a wild and beautiful energy that she allowed to flow through her, without guilt, without hesitation.

In the months since her journey began, she had become a different woman—one who embraced the full spectrum of her existence. She was a mother who no longer strove for perfection in every moment, but instead, showed up with love, authenticity, and the freedom to make mistakes. She was a daughter who had healed old wounds, learning to see her parents as people with their own struggles, their own histories, and finding a deeper connection with them. And she was a woman who had learned that her worth didn't come from what she could give to others, but from how she loved herself.

Her relationship with her children had transformed, too. The old patterns of control and expectation had softened, replaced by a deeper sense of mutual respect. She no longer sought to shape them into versions of herself but instead allowed them the freedom to grow into their own selves, unique and unburdened by her hopes or fears. They, too, had witnessed her evolution, and it was reflected in the way they interacted with her—more freely, more honestly, more openly.

And then there was her marriage. The dynamic between her and her husband had blossomed in ways she hadn't thought possible. Once, they had been two people navigating life together, but now, they were partners—independent, yet deeply connected. They allowed each other to evolve, to be different people with different dreams, without the need for approval or constant validation. They had learned to communicate with vulnerability, to hold space for each other's struggles and victories, and to celebrate the joy of simply being together.

Aradhana's relationships had deepened, but the most profound change had come from within. She had discovered that love was not something she had to earn or strive for—it was simply the energy that flowed through her when she was truly aligned with herself. And from this place of love, everything else fell into place. She no longer felt the need to constantly prove herself or seek approval from others. She had become her own biggest supporter, her own greatest ally.

Looking back at the path she had walked, Aradhana could see how far she had come. The woman who once lived in the shadows of fear, obligation, and perfectionism was now the woman who danced freely in the light of her own truth. She had shed the heavy armor of expectations and replaced it with the lightness of being—authentic, imperfect, wild, and sacred.

The world around her still moved fast, still expected so much, but she no longer measured her worth by those external standards. She knew now that life was not about meeting a certain expectation or achieving a specific outcome. It was about living fully, in every moment, with the grace to embrace what came and the courage to let go of what didn't serve her.

As Aradhana stepped forward, the dance of freedom called her. She had learned that there was no final destination, no ultimate achievement to be unlocked. There was only the journey—unfolding, wild, sacred, and untamed. And she was ready to embrace every step of it.

Reflections and Practical Insights:

- Are you allowing yourself to embrace both your structured and spontaneous sides, or are you suppressing one for the other?
- In what areas of your life are you still seeking external validation instead of trusting your own worth?
- How can you create deeper, more authentic connections by letting go of control and embracing vulnerability?
- What expectations are weighing you down, and how can you release them to live more freely?
- Are you showing up for yourself with the same love and compassion that you offer to others?

How to:

- **Balance Structure and Flow** – Allow space for both discipline and spontaneity in your daily life.
- **Release the Need for Approval** – Practice self-validation by recognizing your worth beyond achievements.
- **Foster Authentic Relationships** – Let go of the need to control outcomes and embrace honest communication.
- **Redefine Success** – Shift your focus from perfection to personal fulfillment and growth.
- **Prioritize Self-Love** – Cultivate daily practices that nurture and affirm your inner well-being.

Mantra:
"I am both sacred and untamed, and I am enough."

Until Next Time..

Acknowledgments

This book is a reflection of the journeys we all take: the ones we stumble through, rise from, and ultimately embrace. To everyone who has walked alongside me, inspired me, and held space for my growth, thank you. Your love, support, and belief in me have been the foundation upon which She Who Stands -Sacred & Untamed has been built.

About the Author

Pragati Mishra is a writer, seeker, and storyteller who believes in the power of authenticity and self-discovery. Through her words, she hopes to inspire women to embrace their strength, vulnerability, and truth. She Who Stands is a celebration of the wild and sacred within every woman, a perspective to the journey of becoming whole. She has been on a learning journey since she a child, and has always had perspectives that were to atleast be Food for thought!

The 13 Mantras of She Who Stands - Sacred & Untamed:

These mantras are a reminder that strength and freedom come from within, that embracing both our sacred and untamed selves is the path to true fulfillment.

1. **"I am not here to fit. I am here to be free."**
2. **"I release the weight of expectations. I choose to honor my truth."**
3. **"I embrace my wildness, for in it lies my strength."**
4. **"I honor my truth and demand the respect that is my birthright."**

5. "I release control and trust in the flow of life."
6. "I forgive not because they deserve it, but because I do."
7. "I am worthy of my own love, every single day."
8. "Every no I say is a yes to my well-being."
9. "I release what no longer serves me, and in doing so, I make space for the life I am meant to live."
10. "Change is the canvas of my life; each stroke is an opportunity to grow, evolve, and embrace the unknown."
11. "I am deserving of love and kindness, especially from myself."
12. "Perfection is a myth. Progress is the truth."
13. "In embracing both the sacred and the untamed within me, I create a life that is whole, authentic, and free."

A Final Note

To the woman reading these words: You are both sacred and untamed, and you are enough. Let this book be your reminder to stand tall, to embrace your journey, and to trust in the unfolding of your path. May you walk forward with courage, authenticity, and the belief that you are meant for more.

My instagram is **Her_ownhero.**
"May the bridges we burn, lights the way for us"
With love and strength,
Pragati Mishra